ISBN: 979-8-9945604-0-2
Published by: Jessika Wheatley
Printed in the United States of America

I0151444

DEDICATION

To my grandfather, Jessie Cooley. Thank you for teaching me the importance of being the same in private as I am in public. You were the example, and I carry that with me.

ACKNOWLEDGEMENTS

First and always, to God —
Thank you for your favor and unlimited grace. Thank you for blessing me even when I was not being intentional and was operating in the worst version of myself. Thank you for never withdrawing your presence, even when I appeared polished, accomplished, and successful on the outside, yet still had work to do within. Thank you for your patience as I learned to align, grow, and become.

To my husband, Darren —
Thank you for your patience, steadiness, and unwavering love. Thank you for understanding me even when I struggle to find the words to express myself. Thank you for recognizing what I need before I know how to ask. Thank you for standing with me without requiring an explanation and for loving me in ways that allow me to be fully and authentically myself. Thank you for supporting all of me, not only the parts that benefit you and our family.

And to my children, Jarren and DJ —
You are my reason, my heart, and the beginning of what I once believed might have been an ending. Everything I build is with you in mind. This work exists to ensure your starting point will always be stronger than mine — so you never have to start from scratch.

Author's Note

This book wasn't written because I finally figured everything out. I honestly doubt I ever will.

It was written because I finally stopped waiting to.

For a long time, I believed I needed more clarity, more time, more credentials, and more certainty before I could put words to paper. I told myself I'd write after the chaos settled… after I felt fully prepared… after I became some polished version of myself that always seemed just out of reach.

But I learned something life-changing: clarity doesn't come before movement — it comes from it.

So I wrote anyway.

This book was written in real moments — in between responsibilities, in quiet pockets of time, and in a season of reflection and recalibration. It was written while I was still figuring it out, still learning, still adjusting… and that is intentional. Because the women I wrote this for don't live in perfect conditions. They live in real life. And real life rarely gives you a clean calendar and a calm mind at the same time.

You won't find perfection here.
You won't find formulas pretending to fix everything.
You won't find a performance.

What you *will* find is honesty.

This book is about legacy — not the kind that looks good on paper, but the kind that endures real life. The kind that holds up under pressure. The kind that survives seasons. The kind that stays standing even when life gets loud. It's the legacy built through alignment, intention, and design — the kind that makes room for mistakes, growth, faith, humor, and rest.

I wrote this for women who are capable… but tired.
For women who are building quietly.
For women who are raising families, carrying responsibility, and still hearing that inner voice whisper, *There has to be more than just surviving.*

There is.

But it doesn't come from hustling harder.
It comes from designing better.
From becoming an intentional architect — not only of your finances, but of your time, your values, your boundaries, and your peace.

As you read, take what resonates and leave what doesn't. There is no pressure to agree with everything here. My hope isn't that you follow my path — but that you feel empowered enough to design your own.

You'll also notice I don't lead with titles. That's intentional.

I've worn many roles and carried many labels — some good, some painful, some probably true — but I've lived inside enough boxes to know they never fully tell the story. In these pages, I'm simply Jessika. Just me. No qualifiers. No performance. No attempt to fit into something smaller or more palatable than I am.

This book comes from that same place — rooted, honest, and unedited.

So, I invite you to read this like a conversation rather than a curriculum. I'm not here to talk down to you. I'm not here to "teach" you like you're behind. I'm here to share what I've lived and learned in the hope that it helps you move with more intention, more clarity, and more compassion for yourself.

And as you read, I want you to imagine I'm sitting across from you, saying this:

You're not late.
You're not broken.
You're not failing.

You're in process.

And most of all... you're not desperate. You were designed — designed with patience and care. Which means you deserve to move through your life with the same patience and care toward yourself.

If this book helps you pause, reflect, realign, or see yourself with a little more compassion and a lot more grace... then it's done its job.

Introduction

Let me say this gently — and then I'll say it plainly.

If motivation worked, most women wouldn't be exhausted.

Motivation is simply a feeling — and unfortunately, feelings fluctuate. Building a life on something that fluctuates is exactly how burnout sneaks in, wearing a productivity planner. Especially the kind designed to appeal to those of us who believe organization, planning, and a cute pen to match the aesthetics are enough to keep us moving forward.

But most advice aimed at women assumes one thing: that if you're not moving forward, it's because you're not trying hard enough.

And I don't believe that.

I believe most women are constantly trying — just without systems that support real life.

Before I explain the logic behind this, let me candidly say: I'm an African American woman — in the almighty America — and my thoughts are backed by my experiences at different points in my life, across different roles: from grade school, to college, the military, and even in corporate systems.

And I'm not saying this for "invisible clout" — the kind that patriarchy and racism have worked together to invent as a way to shift blame and avoid the truth. I'm saying it to establish context rather than content.

Because moving forward, this means that I learned early how systems work — not because I was curious, but because I had to (if you know, you know). And when you don't automatically benefit from the benefit of the doubt, you learn quickly what's written, what's unwritten, and what actually moves outcomes.

And let me add this:

When you're raised by a single mother who spent the majority of her life working in corporate America, you don't have the privilege of growing up believing motivation is enough. Instead, I grew up understanding that consistency, structure, and credibility mattered — sometimes more than enthusiasm ever could.

That awareness didn't make me bitter. It made me precise.

And although it took some time — more than I'd like to admit — it later helped me transition from survival into a space of mental clarity that's grounded in the certainty that drives my ability to now thrive.

So yes, I've thrived — but I'm humble enough to avoid pretending, or even passively implying, it's because limitations didn't exist. I simply refused to let them dictate the ceiling.

Because when you understand systems early, you stop taking things personally… and you start designing around reality.

That's not survival stress framed as resilience to make it palatable. That's strategy. That's what opens the door to success because of — not despite — your limitations.

Now that we have that out of the way, I'm ready to get down in the weeds — be real or clock that tea — as they say.

And trust me when I say: this is worth drinking.

Sis, Motivation Is Not a Strategy

I'll be the first to admit that motivation is great for starting things.

Now hold your breath for this one: it's terrible at sustaining them.

You don't need motivation to brush your teeth, show up for your kids, or pay your bills. Yet when it comes to purpose, income, or identity, we're told to "just stay inspired."

That advice is laziness.

And I personally believe it undermines women's emotions, which are inherently rooted in our lived experiences, no matter how they present themselves. I find it insulting... even disrespectful... because that advice is so commonly thrown at women facing real problems, yet it offers no real solutions.

Here's the problem: motivation assumes unlimited energy.

Real life does not.

Between work, marriage, kids, mental health, responsibilities, and just being human, motivation is unreliable at best.

That's why I don't build around motivation.

I build around a network of systems that support everyday life and habits.

Because motivators inspire action… but architects design outcomes.

Motivators get you excited — and excitement is nice — but is it sustainable? Is it beneficial to your long-term goals?

That's the part people don't tell you.

Motivators ask, *"How do we get people moving?"* Architects ask, *"What happens when they stop?"*

So, to those of you who have politely — intentionally, or maybe even passively — joined the audience to read, criticize, or grow… do me a favor and ask yourself:

Have you ever started something strong and disappeared quietly? Blamed yourself for losing momentum? Wondered why consistency feels harder for you than it seems to be for everyone else?

You don't have to answer aloud.

As a matter of fact, you don't even have to carry secret shame in this moment. I'm not here to be an external source of conviction — but a voice that can speak honestly about my own shortcomings, to open the door for somebody else to succeed.

But first, you have to understand something:

This conversation is not meant to fix you. It's here to tell you the truth.

And the first truth is this:

You were never meant to rely on motivation in the first place.

And if it's not motivation we've been relying on… then sis, let's talk about what we've been surviving on: **hustle**.

Chapter 1

Hustle Is a Trauma Response...Not a Plan

Most women don't hustle because they're ambitious. They hustle because at some point, slowing down wasn't safe. Maybe it was financial. Maybe it was emotional. Maybe it was relational. Maybe it was survival.

But let's admit this once and for all: hustle didn't start as a personality trait. It started as a solution. And for a while, I'm sure it worked.

Hustle Isn't Discipline — It's Conditioning

Hustle teaches you how to move fast. It does not teach you how to rest without guilt. It rewards urgency. It punishes pause. And eventually, it convinces you that exhaustion is evidence of commitment.

And I don't mean to hurt your feelings when I say this, because I get it — trust me. But hustle is not discipline, sis. Now pull yourself together and say this with me — it's conditioning.

Hustle is reactive. It responds to pressure. To fear. To instability. To the sense that if you stop, everything falls apart. And for the women who have carried responsibility early, hustling makes sense.

For women who've been the safety net, hustling feels normal. For women who've lived without true security, hustling feels necessary.

Necessity Is Not a Strategy

But let's keep it real: necessity is not a strategy.

This becomes more apparent when you finally have the strength, time, and courage to evaluate your circumstances — because that's normally when you begin to realize hustle eventually fails you.

And this is why.

Hustle depends on constant output and emotional adrenaline. It uses urgency as fuel. Then, after it has presented itself as a means to a desirable end… it collapses.

Why?

Maybe your energy fluctuated. Your life got fuller. Burdens got heavier. Bills increased. Your capacity changed. Or better yet, your priorities began to shift.

And unfortunately, when the hustle collapses, women don't blame the system — we blame ourselves.

The truth is, we are not always taught the risks of building something that requires constant force.

No One Teaches Us to Be Architects

No one teaches us to be architects, only hustlers.

Architecture Is the Antidote

What is architecture, and why does it matter?

To start, architecture doesn't ignore effort. It redirects it. Instead of asking, *"How much more can I do?"* architecture asks, *"What can I design once so it doesn't require me every time?"*

Architecture puts us in the mode of thinking proactively, so we don't always have to react. It's how we build — not just what we build.

And in this case, what we're building is determined by what we've defined as a means to an end:

Freedom.
Financial freedom.
Freedom   of   time.
Freedom to be moms, wives, and anything we desire to be — without the stress associated with the cost of simply being.

Realizing that being an architect beats hustle — and could place me in a space to thrive rather than survive — helped me to understand that what I really needed to build were systems.

In fact, I'm still building them.

And this is why: systems replace stress, and the structure those systems sit on replaces urgency. When I learned that hustle doesn't always lead to lasting assets, I started focusing on longevity. On building a legacy — something hustle cannot provide for me.

Eventually, I learned that gaining assets — the kind that stand the test of time — also replaces exhaustion.

And by no means am I aiming to be lazy. This isn't about laziness, and I don't want to appear as if I'm promoting it. Especially with how the term *lazy* has been used to classify "**us**" when we start speaking up about fatigue.

But before I go down that rabbit hole... let me make my case in point.

This is about honesty.

It's about exposure — and sharing — to help the masses, because hustle tends to be loud. But I want to shift the focus to legacy.

And with all due respect... legacy is quiet.

Yes, that initially stung me, too — but I permitted myself to carry on because, although this is a conversation for you, this is my book, so I'm moving forward.

Legacy Doesn't Need Applause

Hustle needs applause, while legacy needs something deeper.

Legacy requires alignment rather than performance. Legacy compounds, while hustle only burns hot and fast. Legacy may be slow... but legacy can survive seasons you can't control.

And since you're already knee-deep in your feelings, let me kindly add this:

If hustle could actually build the life you wanted, you'd already be there.

While you're gathering your thoughts and processing how to swallow this, I want to add: I'm not here to shame hustle. I'm here to tell you the truth.

Because hustle may help you survive — but it will not help you scale your way into freedom… or a soft life.

But a change of perspective and focus will.

Chapter 2

Focused, Not Isolated

"You've Been Quiet..."

There's a season when people start saying things like: *"You've been quiet."* *"You   disappeared."* *"You've been hard to reach lately."*

Because we've been taught to hear that as a warning, like pulling back automatically means something is wrong. Like distance equals disconnection. Like focus equals selfishness.

I don't agree, because I believe that this is usually right when something important is taking shape. When dreams are finally starting to become reality. When moves are being made. When your undivided attention is needed for you to reach the next level.

Sometimes You're Not Isolated — You're Focused

Sometimes you're not isolated — you're focused.

Isolation   is   disconnection   without   intention. Focus is connection with boundaries.

While one drains you, the other protects what's being built. And the difference matters — especially for women who are used to being accessible by default.

Now go ahead and raise your hand if this is you. And not the one with the wine glass in it.

Why Access Is Expensive

Here's a truth most women don't say:

Access costs energy.

Every conversation, every explanation, and every opinion invited too early costs you something. And when you're in the early stages of building — an idea, a shift, a new identity — too much access can collapse momentum before it stabilizes.

Not always because people are malicious — but because unfinished things are fragile.

So, it's not a matter of secrecy. It's intentional containment.

And to keep it real: the stresses of everyday life by themselves are enough to make you shut down. But when you're shifting gears to better yourself — aiming to be a legacy builder rather than an exhausted and overstimulated hustler — the need to limit people's access to you only increases.

Unfortunately, high-capacity women are often punished for needing quiet. This is the point where you begin to be labeled "different."

Well, good — because different is usually the first sign that something is being designed instead of reacted to.

It's the point where we stop chasing temporary advances, and our definite aim — our goals — becomes attached to finding infinite sources of provision.

And then we realize: focus is finite.

Therefore, it requires protection.

Focus Is a Finite Resource

Focus isn't infinite. Neither is emotional bandwidth.

For women like me who manage ADHD, depression, anxiety — and just a full life — focus has to be treated like capital, not something you casually spend everywhere.

You Don't Owe Everyone the Blueprint Stage

You don't owe everyone access to the blueprint stage.

Blueprints are messy. They require revision. And they don't need commentary.

Once I learned that, I learned to protect my goals the same way I protect my peace: by limiting access until they can stand on their own.

That doesn't make me antisocial — it makes me intentional.

And that can be difficult for people who are accustomed to having easy, constant access to you.

The Myth of Constant Availability

I think some people have confused availability with virtue.

Being reachable is not the same as being aligned. Being responsive is not the same as being present. Being visible is not the same as being effective.

Focus requires you to be attached to people who understand that — and it limits your ability to communicate with those who don't.

It asks a different question:

"What deserves my attention now — and what can wait?"

And sometimes the answer disappoints people who benefited from your constant availability. They perceive it as cruelty because they don't understand that it's recalibration.

They don't understand recalibration is what's required for you to expand and build a new foundation.

And guess what?

No one builds a house by inviting the neighborhood into the framing stage.

You	build	quietly.
You	reinforce	the	structure.
You	test	the	load.

And only then do you open the doors.

If you're in a season where you're quieter, more selective, more inward — you don't need to explain yourself. You're not disappearing. You're preparing.

This chapter exists because too many women abandon focus out of guilt. They give access too early, dilute ideas too soon, and exhaust themselves explaining something that hasn't fully formed yet.

Focus Without Abandonment

Now, let me be clear about something before it gets misunderstood.

I don't believe in disappearing on the people I love.

I hate when friends vanish without so much as a *"thinking of you"* or a quick check-in. Not because I need constant conversation — I don't — but because silence without intention feels like disconnection, not focus.

That's not how I move.

My inner circle is the circle that I'm in alignment with. Those relationships don't disappear when my attention shifts. The patterns don't change — only the rhythm does.

So even if I retreat to work and go quiet for a stretch, the line stays open.

I still manage to send a text, a voice note, or a quick *"hey sis, just thinking of you"* — because I'm an adult. I manage my time like I manage my expectations. And I understand the importance of effort, and how it shapes relationships.

Therefore, when I resurface, the connection is still there — not because it was maintained through constant access, but because it was grounded in alignment.

Focus requires honest pacing — but it does not require abandonment.

Precision Builds Legacy

Remember this:

Focus isn't isolation. It's precision. And precision is how architecture holds. And architecture is what takes us from being laborers… to legacy builders.

CHAPTER 3

Labor vs. Legacy

When Focus Reveals the Truth

Once you start protecting your focus, something interesting happens: you notice how much of your life is built around output — not ownership.

You start wondering why you're busy, needed, and relied on… and still, nothing feels like it lasts. That's usually the moment you begin to evaluate what you're actually building — not just for today, or even this year, but over time.

But, here's the thing: you can be focused, disciplined, and exhausted — all at the same time.

Focus alone doesn't guarantee legacy. It just gives you the space to finally see the difference between labor and what comes after it.

Labor   keeps   things   moving.
Legacy keeps them standing.

And you start saying things like: *"I don't look down on work — I come from it."*

Labor Has a Ceiling

I, for one, watched hard work growing up. I lived it — and I still do it. Because labor is honest. It's necessary. It's how bills get paid, and families stay afloat.

But labor has a ceiling because it is tied directly to:

- how much time you have
- how much energy you can give
- how available you are
- how well your body and mind cooperate

So, when you stop laboring, your labor stops paying.

And although that doesn't make labor bad, it does make it temporary. And temporary effort, repeated forever, is how burnout disguises itself as responsibility.

It is not how you build a legacy.

Legacy Is What Survives Your Absence

Legacy starts when something you built doesn't collapse the moment you step away.

It's not mystical. It's not reserved for rich people or people with fancy titles. It's simply anything you designed once that continues to create value without demanding you every single time.

Legacies can be:

- knowledge you finally decided to structure instead of keeping in your head

- systems you stopped recreating from scratch

- ideas you documented instead of repeating

- assets that don't require your constant presence

No matter how they're framed, legacies are designed to pay it forward.

Labor Is Paid Once. Legacy Pays Forward.

This was the shift that changed how I think about effort:

Labor is paid once. Legacy pays forward.

When we trade time for money, the exchange ends when the time does. But when you build something reusable — a system, a framework, a piece of intellectual property — it keeps working after the effort is done.

This is not greed. This is foresight.

And foresight is something women are rarely taught to prioritize — which is why women stay in labor mode.

Why Women Stay in Labor Mode

It has been my personal experience that women are taught to be useful first... and strategic later — if ever.

We're rewarded for being: dependable, responsible, available — the one who holds it all together.

I'm quite frankly exhausted with this tired and dated philosophy, and I'm sure many of you can agree.

And if you're a Black woman, I'm going to say something you already know — and I'm going to say it without making it dramatic:

A lot of us grew up learning how to stretch, rather than how to invest.

We learned how to pay the bills, how not to get the lights cut off, how to save for a rainy day, how to be responsible — and my all-time favorite: the importance of working twice as hard.

And listen, just to be clear: that *is* financial knowledge. That's survival intelligence.

But be for real — survival intelligence doesn't automatically turn into wealth strategy.

Not because women are incapable, but because access to the next level of information isn't distributed evenly. We're kept out of "the know", so we never get to "do".

Now consider how many women are taught to save rather than invest. Saving is framed as "safe," and investing is framed as "risky." Further emphasizing that "safe" is the only way to protect our future.

But what they don't teach us is this: when you combine that mindset with lower income over time, it becomes harder to participate in higher-return assets in the first place.

Provision vs. Autonomy

I'd like to highlight that this conversation also applies to a group that's often invisible in financial discussions:

Married women who still feel like single parents.

In all fairness, this may not be because their husbands aren't present or because they aren't provided for — but because the weight of daily responsibility still lands on their shoulders.

And then some stay-at-home mothers are deeply grateful for provision… and still quietly unsettled by the fact that they don't generate income of their own.

Both realities can exist at the same time.

And to be frank: when you don't earn money directly, it can change how you experience power — even in a healthy marriage.

You may not question your value out loud, resent your partner, or want to trade roles.

Yet still, something shifts internally when your labor isn't financially visible.

That doesn't mean you're ungrateful. It means you're human.

And another truth became clear to me:

Provision and autonomy are not the same thing.

Being taken care of doesn't automatically translate into feeling secure, seen, or self-directed — especially for women who are capable, thoughtful, and used to contributing beyond caretaking.

When all your effort goes into holding the household together, and none of it produces income you can point to, identity can start to blur.

Not because motherhood or partnership lacks value — but because self-worth is sometimes still (inadvertently) connected to financial freedom for some women.

This is where legacy thinking matters — not to replace anyone's role, but to restore internal balance.

Legacy isn't about competing with your partner. It's about maintaining ownership over yourself.

It's about knowing that if circumstances changed — even temporarily — you wouldn't lose your footing, your voice, or your sense of capability.

And before some of you lose your mind and spit your wine out in disgust, please know: I'm not here to tell married women they should "do more," or stay-at-home moms that they need to monetize everything.

I'm here to provide a safe space to have this conversation — a space that aims to eliminate the anxiety attached to the fears and discomfort that come up when discussing these topics in other places.

Legacy Work Looks Selfish First

Therefore, when I say, *"labor is paid once, legacy pays forward,"* I'm not talking down to anybody.

I'm saying many of us were trained for responsibility — not ownership.

So, whether you're Black, White, Latina, Asian, immigrant, first-gen, married, single, corporate, or home with kids…

If your financial education stopped at *"be careful,"* you can still learn to build.

And let me add this:

Legacy work often looks selfish before it looks smart — especially when people are used to having unlimited access to you.

So instead of building assets, women tend to build endurance.

But endurance eventually turns into exhaustion — not because we're weak, but because no one taught us differently.

And sometimes, when you begin speaking like this, it feels like people label the conversation as "escape."

However, legacy doesn't require you to run—not from your career, and not from the life you're living right now.

Legacy requires design.

Legacy isn't something you run off to find. It's something you build right where you are, with what you have, in the season you're in. You don't have to quit your job, disappear, or start over to become who you were called to be. Sometimes, legacy looks like showing up, standing tall, and refusing to shrink in environments that were never designed to fully hold you. Because the truth is—your purpose can live in the middle of your everyday life.

It's a layering strategy — something that can be built quietly, alongside your responsibilities.

The Question That Changes Everything

When labor is centered around how much more we can do, it can be a hard left turn towards legacy thinking, which asks how we can design in a way that doesn't require constant effort.

It can be difficult adjusting to the concept of "passive" after we've been taught that labor is what sustains us and gives us purpose.

But once you get to the point where you're over it — where you've had enough — you become open.

And that is when your relationship with time begins to change.

That is when your tolerance for the waste of energy, effort, and *yourself* significantly decreases.

Chapter 4

Money Will Act Up Worse Than a Man If You Don't Tell It What to Do

Money is not emotional — but it will absolutely react to chaos. And if you don't give it direction, it will start freelancing in ways you didn't authorize.

Most people are taught to treat money like a reward: you work hard, you survive the week, you exhale… and then you spend.

And listen, that makes sense when you've carried responsibility, gone without, or lived in survival mode. I'm not here to shame relief.

But relief and strategy are not the same thing.

When money doesn't have a job, it will always find one for you — usually in the form of impulse spending, emergency scrambling, or lifestyle creep that quietly convinces you that you "deserve" everything in your cart.

Money without instruction will act up every single time.

Unassigned Money Is Undisciplined Money

I had to learn this the hard way.

I don't eat my stress — I shop it.

I		shop		when		I'm		bored.
I		shop		when		I'm		upset.
I		shop		when		I'm		happy.
I	shop	when	the	kids	are	stressing	me	out.

I shop when my husband pisses me off.

Girl, if there is an emotion, there is a store that will happily take my money and tell me I earned it.

And for a long time, I confused emotional regulation with retail therapy. And to be transparent, sometimes I still relapse and make the mistake of doing so.

What I had to confront wasn't that I was irresponsible — it was that I was unassigned.

My money was moving faster than my intentions.

Awareness Before Restraint

One of the habits I had to build was awareness before restraint.

I still go into stores. I still browse. I still pick things up. But now, I give myself time — real time — to reconnect with my financial goals, what I call my definite chief aims. Before I buy anything, I take a moment to think. I picture the goals I wrote down. I picture the debt I'm paying off. I picture the savings I'm building.

And then I ask myself one question: *Does this purchase support who I'm becoming?*

If it doesn't, I put it back — not because I can't afford it, but because I'm choosing alignment, so I remind myself why I'm building what I'm building, and then give myself permission to put things back.

Sometimes I leave with nothing. Sometimes I leave with only what I came for. And sometimes — let's be honest — I still buy something.

But the difference is intention.

My husband knows this routine so well that he'll intentionally linger in the store, hoping I'll snap back into reality and start returning things aisle by aisle.

And sometimes… he's right. At other times, his wishful thinking is just that… a wish.

Peace Comes From Alignment

This chapter isn't about never spending money.

I love nice things. I love experiences. I love to travel. I love enjoying the life I'm working hard to build.

But I also love peace.

And peace doesn't come from pretending money management is about discipline alone. It comes from alignment.

Money works best when it's treated like a tool — not a trophy.

When you assign it a job before it ever leaves your hands — savings, investing, travel, debt reduction, legacy building — you stop being surprised by where it goes. You stop arguing with yourself later. You stop feeling like you're always one bad month away from unraveling.

Systems Make Room for Real Life

This matters even more for women — especially women who were never taught to invest, only to save.

Many of us were taught to be careful, not powerful. To hold money, not multiply it. To make do, not design.

And when you layer that with pay disparities, caregiving responsibilities, and seasons where simply surviving took everything you had… it's not that you failed financially. It's that you were carrying more than most people ever see. You were doing the best you could with what you had, while still showing up for everybody else. And the world loves to label that as "poor decisions," without acknowledging the pressure, the sacrifice, or the invisible work.

So no, you didn't fail. You were stretched. You were responsible for too much, with too little support, and still expected to make it look easy.

It's that you were operating without systems.

Whether you're a single mother trying to make it, a married woman who still feels like she's carrying everything alone, or a stay-at-home mom whose household is provided for, but whose identity feels invisible — money plays a role in self-worth whether we admit it or not.

And that's exactly why financial stability is deeper than numbers. It's not just about what's in your account — it's about what it represents: safety, choice, breathing room, and the ability to show up for your family without losing yourself in the process.

When money is tight, it can feel like your worth is tight too. But when you have a plan — when you've built systems — money stops being a constant source of fear and starts becoming a tool you can actually use with confidence.

There were seasons when I carried my entire household financially. When my husband was injured and unable to work, I paid the bills and still took my kids on a nice vacation — not because I was reckless, but because I was prepared.

And that preparation didn't come from earning more. It came from intentionally assigning my money a job long before the crisis showed up.

That's the quiet power of systems: they don't eliminate life's disruptions, but they soften the impact — so you don't have to panic your way through them.

And that right there is the difference between *looking* free and *being* free. Because you can catch a flight, take a cute picture, and still be stressed the entire time. You can be in a whole new country and still be mentally tied to unpaid bills, unstable routines, and a life that depends on you doing everything.

That's why travel isn't the proof — structure is.

Travel Isn't the Proof

Travel, for my closest friends and me, is a love language. It's how we reconnect, decompress, bond, laugh, heal, and just be free to speak honestly.

But even travel feels heavy when you're still operating in a labor mindset instead of a systems mindset. Because you don't just "take a trip." You do labor before the trip, labor during the trip, and labor after the trip. You're the planner, the problem-solver, the caretaker, the packer, the budgeter, the reminder system, the calendar, the backup plan. So even when you're supposed to be relaxing, you're still working — just in a different location.

That's not a vacation. That's relocation.

And girl, let's be real. You don't need a passport to feel behind. You can be right in your hometown and still feel like life is passing you by. All it takes is one Instagram scroll—one minute you're minding your business, the next minute you're questioning your whole life because somebody you went to high school with is in Dubai, engaged, glowing, and holding a drink you can't pronounce.

Meanwhile, you're budgeting groceries, paying bills, and praying nothing unexpected hits your bank account. And that's when you realize: it's not always the travel that gets you…it's the comparison.

Behind isn't always about location—it's about pressure. It's watching people hit milestones while you're still recovering from the seasons that took everything out of you. Some of us weren't building for a while—we were surviving. So don't compare your survival season to somebody else's highlight reel.

You don't have to be on a plane to feel the pressure to catch up. Sometimes you just need a timeline you keep measuring yourself against. But hear me: late doesn't mean lost. And behind doesn't mean you're not on your way. Because comparison is already a trip… and it'll take you places you never needed to go.

And if you can't travel right now, that doesn't mean you're failing. It means you're in a season. A season where your priorities might be different. A season where stability matters more than stamps in a passport.

 And mature people understand seasons—they understand that sometimes you save instead of spend, build instead of browse, and regroup instead of run.

You're not stuck—you're preparing. You're not behind—you're building. You're not missing out—you're making sure when you *do* go, you can enjoy it without stress, without guilt, and without coming home to chaos.

This may be a season where you're choosing responsibility over applause, healing over escape, and peace over proving something to people who aren't paying your bills anyway. So give yourself grace. Some seasons are for exploring, and some are for establishing—but every season has purpose.

The goal isn't to *look* free. The goal is to *be* free. And freedom takes planning. Not escape. Alignment. Because when you're aligned, you stop chasing what looks good and start choosing what *is* good.

You stop making decisions based on what people will clap for, and you start making decisions based on what your future will thank you for. Alignment teaches you how to move with intention — not impulse. And when you live like that, freedom stops being a fantasy and starts becoming your lifestyle.

So remember this, travel is a reward — not the proof.

The proof is what you do on the regular days. The proof is your ability to stay aligned when life is loud, when you're tired, when everybody needs something from you, and when rest still has to be fought for. Because alignment isn't just a mindset — it's a practice. It's the decisions you make when nobody's watching and the systems you put in place, so your goals don't depend on your mood.

That's why the next principle matters so much: Balance Isn't Quiet.

Balance Isn't Quiet

And alignment doesn't mean perfection.

I still sit in my car outside the garage for thirty minutes to an hour when I get home, hoping my youngest doesn't interrupt my decompression time.

I still juggle homework, cleaning, checking in with friends, and making sure the house doesn't fall apart.

And just when I think I'm finally headed upstairs for peace… I hear music playing — *that music* — my husband's "I'm ready to get busy" playlist.

And I cringe a little, because I love that man dearly… and I'm also very aware that I still have to take care of him too. But when you're exhausted, it takes an extra push.

But the thing about balance is realizing you can be deeply in love and still sigh before you rally.

Balance is laughing at yourself, turning the music down just a notch, and remembering that you're a wife… and a woman who's been managing everybody's needs all day.

What saves you isn't willpower. It's design.

Systems save you from yourself. They create structure when emotions run high. They hold the vision when motivation dips.

And when it comes to money, the system is simple:

Assign it a job — or it will assign one for you. Every time.

Chapter 5

Why Nobody Told Us This Was a Team Sport

The Family as an Economic Unit

After talking about money, it would be easy to stop there — to treat finances like a solo responsibility or a personal character trait.

But money doesn't live in isolation.

It moves through households, relationships, and decisions long before it ever shows up in a bank account. How money behaves in your life is deeply connected to how your family operates, communicates, and adapts.

Whether we acknowledge it or not, family is the first system most of us ever belong to — and it quietly shapes how we earn, spend, save, give, and survive.

So, before we talk about building wealth, we have to talk about the environment money actually lives in.

Default vs. Intention

Let's keep this conversational, because the moment we make family sound like a boardroom, everybody checks out.

When I talk about the family as an economic unit, I'm not talking about turning your house into a corporation or handing out performance reviews at the dinner table. I'm naming something most of us are already living — but haven't named.

Money, time, energy, labor, decisions… they're already moving through your household every single day.

Therefore, the question isn't whether your family is an economic unit.

The question is whether it's operating with intention… or on default.

Unspoken Systems Benefit Someone

Every family already has systems, even when we pretend they don't.

Who		pays			what?
Who		remembers			what?
Who	carries	the	mental		load?
Who	adjusts	when	life		shifts?

Who handles emergencies?

Some of those systems are spoken — but most of them aren't.

And here's the part nobody likes to say out loud:

Unspoken systems usually benefit one person more than everyone else.

That's not blame — that's math.

Visibility Before Fairness

If you're a woman, this part is familiar.

We plan. We anticipate. We remember. We smooth things over. We make it work quietly.

Even   in   loving   homes.
Even   with   good   partners.
Even when nobody is "doing anything wrong."

And before anyone gets defensive — relax. This isn't about fault. It's about visibility.

Because labor   that   isn't   named   can't   be   shared.
And labor that can't be shared eventually gets heavy.

Unfiltered Truth

And before moving forward, I'd like to be clear: I'm a Black woman talking to all women — and I'm not shrinking my voice to make anyone more comfortable.
Being articulate and being Black are not opposites. Being strategic and being Black are not contradictions.

If this resonates with you, it's because the truth travels — not because I adjusted it.

And the truth is this: Black women have been holding families and stretching resources for generations. What we haven't always had is shared structure and protected continuity.

And when structure isn't shared, someone becomes the default. Someone becomes the stabilizer. Someone becomes the one who adjusts, compensates, and carries what isn't being named. That's why this chapter isn't about blame — it's about building a system that doesn't collapse when roles shift. Because roles *will* shift. And if your partnership can't adapt, the household will eventually break under the silence.

Partnership Is Adaptive (Not 50/50)

Family economics isn't about splitting everything straight down the middle, because partnership isn't fifty-fifty — it's adaptive.

There are seasons when one person earns more. Seasons when one person carries more emotionally. Seasons when one person stabilizes the household. And seasons when roles flip completely.

The problem isn't imbalance. The problem is the silence around it.

Because imbalance isn't always abuse — sometimes it's just life. A layoff. A baby. An injury. Depression. Burnout. A demanding season. And in those moments, somebody naturally has to carry more. The problem is when that shift becomes normal, but nobody names it. Nobody checks in. Nobody renegotiates the agreement. Nobody adjusts expectations or asks, "Are you okay?" And what you don't talk about turns into tension. What you don't name turns into expectation. What you don't address turns into resentment.

Silence doesn't keep peace — it just keeps the pressure hidden until it explodes. That's after the person carrying more starts to feel alone, unseen, and eventually resentful — not because they had to step up, but because they had to step up in silence. Because silence doesn't protect relationships — it protects dysfunction. And eventually the weight you carry quietly becomes the anger you can't hide.

Because when roles shift, and nobody talks about it, resentment fills the gap.

Ask me how I know.

Blending Families Means Inheriting History

I didn't learn this in theory. I learned it while being gone.

The military took me away from my family for several long stretches. My husband was working. We were trying to stay connected while living in different worlds — then trying to find each other again when I came back.

Marriage doesn't pause when life is demanding. It stretches.
And sometimes it stretches you first.

Because being married isn't just about love — it's about continuity. It's about learning how to keep choosing each other while life keeps interrupting you. You don't always get the luxury of stability. Sometimes you're building the foundation while the house is still shaking.

And real life doesn't start on a clean slate.

My husband and I both came into our marriage with kids. Which means we didn't just blend families — we inherited history. Not just birthdays, school schedules, and co-parenting logistics — but emotional residue.

Residue from past relationships. Old habits. Old mistakes. Old assumptions. Unhealed versions of ourselves that still knew how to protect, deflect, shut down, or fight for control.

Assumptions that had nothing to do with the person standing in front of us... but still somehow showed up to the argument.

Because sometimes you're not arguing about what happened today — you're arguing about what *used to* happen. You're reacting to what hurt you before. You're defending yourself from a version of pain that already existed.

And nobody talks enough about how much work it takes to clean up messes you didn't make together.

You're trying to build something new while also undoing what came before it. You're learning each other while also unlearning survival. You're trying to keep the peace while navigating personalities, parenting styles, outside opinions, old wounds, and new expectations.

And it's exhausting because you're doing double work: the work of marriage... and the work of healing.

So you find yourself having to pause and remind yourself:
"Okay... that reaction wasn't really about you."
"Yeah... that response came from a version of me that existed before you."
"Let me not punish you for what someone else did."
"Let me not bleed on you just because I was cut somewhere else."

That extra cleanup doesn't pause the work of marriage — it adds to it. It adds emotional labor. It adds patience. It adds hard conversations you didn't feel like having. It adds the need to constantly check your tone, your triggers, and your tenderness — because the goal isn't just to be right. The goal is to be safe.

So if you ever felt like you were working harder than the situation in front of you required...
Girl, you probably were.

You weren't just dealing with the moment. You were dealing with the history behind it.

And when you inherit history, you don't just inherit what happened — you inherit how people *think*. You inherit what was modeled, what was normalized, and what was never protected. You inherit strengths... and blind spots.

So for us, the goal couldn't just be love. Love alone doesn't raise kids. Love alone doesn't manage schedules. Love alone doesn't keep the lights on. And love alone doesn't undo the residue of what life handed you before you even met each other.

We had to build something stronger than feelings — something transferable. Shared language. Shared systems. Shared thinking. Because in the end, the greatest inheritance isn't just money or property... it's the framework. The strategy. The structure that helps the next generation win faster.

A Unit, Not Competitors

We didn't magically know how to balance each other — or parenting, or partnership.

We experimented.

What   made   us   happy?
What   didn't?
What worked in one season... and absolutely didn't in the next?

We became a couple... then became different versions of ourselves again. We had to unlearn how we were raised and taught ourselves how to parent in alignment with our own values — not just inherited ones.

That process wasn't clean.

It was conversations, disagreements, growth, and adjustment.

Add kids' activities. Sports schedules. Practices and games. Family drama — because let's be honest, that's never optional. Then add life, doing what life does best: interrupting your plans.

And somehow you're still expected to be: emotionally available, financially responsible, mentally present, spiritually grounded…

Girl… that's a lot.

I've lived seasons where I carried my household financially. I paid the bills, handled responsibilities, and still made sure my kids experienced joy.

Not because I wanted control — but because the situation required coverage.

And the reason that season didn't break us is simple:

We understood we were operating as a unit, not competitors.

Preparedness doesn't threaten partnership.

It stabilizes it.

And yes — that kind of confidence is attractive.

Raising Contributors, Not Dependents

When I talk about family as an economic unit, I'm not talking about money first.

I'm talking about capacity.

My goal is for my kids to be able to feed my grandkids off the same plate I fixed.

Not   the   literal   plate   —   but   the   source.
The   thinking   behind   it.
The   systems   behind   it.
The access behind it.

There should be plenty to eat even when their dad and I are gone.

A family becomes powerful when nothing important lives in one person's head.

When   kids   understand   why   decisions   are   made.
When   effort   connects   to   outcome.
When   mistakes   don't   reset   everything.
When knowledge is shared instead of protected.

That's when you stop raising dependents... and start raising contributors.

Not contributors to bills — contributors to continuity.

Legacy Isn't a Lecture — It's Exposure

Legacy isn't a lecture.

It's exposure.

Kids don't need adult stress — absolutely not — but they *can* understand adult thinking.

This	is	how	we	decide.
This	is	how	we	adjust.
This	is	how	we	recover.

This is how we take care of each other.

That's how you raise kids who don't panic when life shifts.

A Table Big Enough

My grandmother Agnes often says, *"It was alright... but it wasn't nothing to take home and brag to mama about."*

That is her way of saying: don't confuse noise with substance. Don't confuse effort with outcome. Don't bring back anything that can't stand on its own when examined closely.

That stayed with me.

Because family as an economic unit doesn't mean rigidity. It means shared language, shared awareness, and shared responsibility.

It   means   no   one   is   operating   in   the   dark.
No   one   is   silently   carrying   everything.
No one is invisible.

There will still be chaos. Still drama. Still tired days.

But when the foundation is shared, the house doesn't collapse just because life gets loud.

That's the kind of legacy worth taking home.

Not   money   hoarded.
Not   pressure   passed   down.
Not expectations without tools.

But a table big enough that the next generation doesn't have to ask if there's room.

Because when you really think about it, the most powerful thing my family ever gave me wasn't something I could hold — it was something I could *use*. It was how to stretch. How to build. How to make a way out of no way.

And once you understand that, you realize something life-changing: inheritance isn't only land, money, or material things. Sometimes the greatest legacy is the knowledge, the strategy, and the framework that keeps producing long after you're gone.

That's why in the next chapter, we're going to talk about a form of inheritance most families overlook — intellectual property. Because when you can own what you know… you can pass down more than survival. You can pass down systems.

Chapter 6

You Can't Leave Them What You Don't Understand

Intellectual Property as Inheritance

Now let's talk about the plate itself. Not the food. Not the table. The source.

Because this is where legacy either multiplies… or quietly dies.

And I'm going to be honest: when most people hear the phrase *intellectual property*, they instantly check out. They picture patents, trademarks, tech companies… or something reserved for people in hoodies with venture capital and a team of lawyers.

Girl, no.

Intellectual property isn't fancy — it's familiar.

It's simply what you know that keeps producing value.

It's what you can do so well that people keep coming back for it. It's what you understand that saves time, saves money, and saves stress. It's what you've learned the hard way — the lessons you paid for in tears, setbacks, trial-and-error, and long nights.

Intellectual property is:

* how you think

- how you solve problems

- how you structure decisions

- how you recover from mistakes

- how you notice patterns

- how you build systems that work more than once

Because let's be real… we all know somebody who has money, but no structure. They might have a good job, a nice car, and decent income — but every emergency wipes them out. Every setback sends them spiraling. They don't have systems, they just have survival.

And survival can't be inherited.

If your children can only inherit *things*, they'll eventually run out. They'll break it, spend it, lose it, mishandle it, or simply outgrow it. And if the foundation isn't there, the "blessing" becomes pressure.

But if they inherit *thinking*… they'll always be able to build again.

They	won't	panic	when	life	shifts.
They	won't	collapse	when	plans	change.

They won't feel like failure is final.

Because they'll know how to rebuild from scratch if they have to. And that right there? That's legacy.

Labor Ends. Thinking Reproduces.

Labor gets paid once. Thinking gets paid repeatedly.

And listen — I'm not knocking labor. I come from it. I respect it. I honor it.

But I had to learn the difference between working hard… and building something that keeps working *without me*.

Because when you work with your body or your time, the value stops when you stop.

If you don't clock in, you don't get paid. If you don't show up, the money doesn't move. If you get sick, injured, overwhelmed, or burned out — the whole system pauses.

That's labor.

But when you build frameworks, processes, systems, and ways of seeing — those outlive you.

That's why intellectual property is inheritance.

Not because it's glamorous… but because it reproduces.

It keeps working long after the original effort is done.

That's the part most people miss

Because some people are leaving their kids:

- a house, but no home training

- money, but no money sense

- nice things, but no discipline

- resources, but no direction

But when you leave them *thinking…* you leave them capacity. You leave them tools. You leave them access.

That's why the real flex isn't "I worked hard."

The   real   flex   is:
"I built something once… and it keeps producing."

That could be:

- a business model you can teach

- a workflow you can repeat

- a process your kids can apply

- a set of rules that protects peace

- a framework that turns chaos into clarity

That's intellectual property.

That's inheritance.

And once you start seeing it that way, you'll stop asking, "What can I leave them?"

You'll start asking the more powerful question:

"What do I understand well enough to pass down?"

I Wasn't Unstable — I Was Learning

I've had multiple LLCs and just as many business ideas. And I know how that can sound to some people — like I'm inconsistent, or can't make up my mind, or don't know what I'm doing.

But I'm not ashamed of it.

Some of my ideas failed. Some didn't fail — I just got bored. Some ended because discipline hadn't caught up to interest yet. Some were casualties of ADHD before I learned how to design around it instead of trying to "power through" it.

And I don't hide that, because I'm not here to pretend I've always had it together. I'm here to tell the truth: progress doesn't always look like one straight line. Sometimes it looks like trying something, learning what you needed to learn, and being brave enough to pivot without shaming yourself for it.

Because iteration isn't instability — it's information.

Every attempt taught me something real:

- what actually held my attention

- what drained me faster than it built me

- what could scale

- what couldn't

- what required structure instead of motivation

And that matters, because the knowledge didn't disappear just because the idea did.

Even the "failed" things left me with something: experience. clarity. strategy. lessons I had to earn. And when you stack those lessons over time, you start to realize you weren't wasting time — you were collecting data. You were learning your rhythm. You were learning your wiring. You were learning what kind of builder you are.

That knowledge transfers.

That's intellectual property.

And once you understand that, you stop treating your past attempts like proof that you can't finish... and you start treating them like proof that you're learning how to build something that lasts.

Systems Saved Me

Interest fades. Motivation lies. Life interrupts. Systems stay.

Once I stopped relying on excitement and started relying on structure, everything changed — not because I became perfect, but because I stopped expecting perfection to carry the load.

I know this because I lived it.

When I was a single mother, I would not have survived if I had depended only on daycare. I could leave my son there eight hours a day… and real life still didn't fit neatly inside that window.

At the same time, I was trying to find my footing — working and rebuilding my life while fighting a divorce and an expensive custody case.

I was fighting for the one thing I was certain about in that season: my oldest son, Jarren Christopher.

That was the anchor.

Daycare helped. But it wasn't enough on its own.

What carried me was the system around me.

My grandparents. My parents. Friends who stepped in. Some of their parents showed up without needing an explanation.

People helped me hold time, space, childcare, sanity, and survival while I figured things out.

That wasn't luck. That wasn't charity.

That was a support system — designed, even if it didn't feel organized at the time.

Interdependence Done Right

And those systems didn't stop once I remarried — they expanded.

With the addition of my mother-in-law, my sweet sister-in-law, and brother-in-law (Charles and Tarsheena) — who are no longer with us but are forever part of this story — that support system became part of the reason I was able to keep going.

Without them:

- I would not have been successful in the military as a recruiter — a high-demand, high-pressure role requiring constant mental endurance

- I would not have earned my associate's degree or gone on to complete the others

- I would not have been able to attend military schools that lasted seven or eight weeks at a time

- I would not have been able to deploy and fulfill my duties to my country

None of that would've been possible without coverage at home.

And yes — I also had a husband who has always been active, present, and just as involved in the care and support of our children as I was, but the additional support was a must.

That mattered. That still matters.

This wasn't independence.

This was interdependence done right.

And without it, I would not have made it — not because I wasn't capable, but because capacity without coverage eventually collapses.

That experience changed how I define strength forever.

Strength isn't doing everything alone. Strength is knowing how to build around yourself, so you don't break.

What I Want My Kids to Inherit

That's what I want my kids to inherit.

Not my hustle.

My architecture.

Your kids don't need a lecture on intellectual property.

They need to see you:

- document your thinking
- build something once and reuse it
- explain your choices
- adjust when things fail
- talk through decisions out loud

That's how thinking becomes legacy — not through pressure, but through proximity.

Money can disappear. Titles expire. Jobs end.

But if your children inherit discernment, structure, adaptability, patience, and systems thinking...

They'll never be empty-handed.

They'll always know how to set another table.

And that is the inheritance nobody can repossess.

CHAPTER 7

Don't Make Them Pay for What You Survived

Teaching Without Transferring Trauma

Here's where a lot of well-meaning women — good mothers, thoughtful partners, and intentional leaders — get it wrong.

We want better for our kids, so we give them everything: information, opportunity, access, expectations… and sometimes pressure. Not because we're harsh, but because we're scared. Scared they'll struggle. Scared they'll be unprepared. Scared they'll fall behind. Scared they'll experience what we had to survive.

But hear me: legacy isn't built by turning children into projects. It's built by raising whole people.

And if we're not careful, the very pain we overcame becomes the weight we place on them. We start parenting from anxiety instead of alignment. We start teaching from fear instead of faith. We start confusing preparation with pressure — and calling it love because our intentions were good.

But intentions don't erase impact.

And this chapter is simple: don't make them pay for what you survived.

Before anyone accuses me of giving parenting advice — because this is far from it — let me be clear: I'm not a parenting expert. I'm a mom. And even after sixteen years of doing this, I'm still learning in real time. Failing in real time. Figuring it out in real time. Really just trying to be the best mom that I can be.

What I *do* know is this: children don't stay still long enough for you to master one version of them before they evolve into another. Just when you think you've figured it out, they change — their needs, their language, their emotions, their boundaries... and you have to adapt again.

Parenting requires constant adjustment. And some days, I struggle to keep up with the demands of who my children are becoming — not because I don't care, but because growth doesn't come with a manual for the next phase.

So if you're reading this hoping for perfection or certainty, that's not what I'm offering. What I'm offering is honesty — and permission to learn as you go.

Exposure vs. Burden

Moving forward, here's the truth:

There's a difference between exposure and burden.

Exposure says, *"Let me show you how this works."* Burden says, *"Now carry it."*

Children don't need to hold adult stress to become capable adults. They need context — not anxiety.

They need to understand how decisions are made... not feel responsible for outcomes they didn't create.

Legacy should feel like security — not obligation.

Confidence Without Perfection

I strongly believe that one of the most powerful lessons you can give a child is simply this:

"I don't know everything — but I know how to figure it out."

Let them see you learn. Let them see you adjusting, changing your mind, resting, saying no, and starting again.

That teaches confidence without arrogance.

It tells them they don't have to be perfect to be capable.

Legacy Isn't Cloning — It's Cultivation

Not every child builds the same way.

Some		lead.
Some		design.
Some	observe	quietly.
Some innovate later.		

Legacy isn't cloning — it's cultivation.

Your job isn't to decide who they become. It's to make sure they're resourced enough to choose.

Protection vs. Control

Sometimes we confuse protection with control.

We hover. We over-explain. We over-schedule. We over-prepare.

But kids don't need to be shielded from everything.

They need to know how to recover… how to ask for help… how to pause… how to regulate… and how to trust themselves.

That's resilience.

Cycles Change Through Structure + Grace

What you're really passing down isn't money or titles.

You're passing down how to think, how to decide, how to recover — and how to build again.

That's what keeps cycles from repeating.

Not   pressure.
Not   fear.
Not *"don't mess this up."*

But structure paired with grace.

The goal isn't to raise children who feel indebted. It's to raise adults who feel equipped — adults who understand systems, who value people, who know when to rest, and who know when to build.

That's how cycles change: not through force, but through freedom anchored in structure.

A Transition Into the Final Chapter

By now, something should feel different.

This   book   hasn't   asked   you   to   hustle   harder.
It   hasn't   asked   you   to   become   perfect.
It hasn't asked you to perform strength.

It's asked you to pay attention to patterns, to cycles, to systems, to alignment.

Which brings us to the final chapter — not an ending, but a completion.

Because everything meaningful moves in cycles.

CHAPTER 8

Why Eight?

Completion, Continuity, and Choosing to Share the Table

If you're wondering why this book ends at eight chapters, you're not alone. That question is intentional — because eight isn't random, it's symbolic.

Eight represents completion with continuity. Not an ending, but a cycle fulfilled. The kind of finish that doesn't shut the door — it strengthens the foundation. Eight reminds us that what's built right doesn't disappear when the page turns.

It becomes a new starting point.

This book isn't proof that I've arrived. It's proof that I've aligned. Aligned with who I am now, aligned with what matters, aligned with what I'm building instead of what I'm reacting to.

For a long time, I couldn't focus long enough to write this book — not because I didn't have the ideas, but because my energy was scattered. Pulled by obligations. Distracted by noise. Frustrated by family drama, trauma, and old cycles that kept trying to reintroduce themselves.

And yes — if you were around back then, which wasn't that long ago, you might've been expecting a very different book. I know... some of y'all were waiting on the tell-all.

Here's the truth: I outgrew that version of myself.

Not because the story wasn't real, but because my spirit shifted. I'm not here to entertain, rehash, or drag old wounds into a new season. I'm here to build forward.

And honestly, peace is way louder than drama ever was.

In fact, the only reason I was able to sit still long enough to write this book is because of my walk with God and an intentional focus and effort on alignment.

Not based on what's happening around me. Not performance. Not pretending.

Alignment.

Learning when to pause, when to move, and when to release what no longer fits. Learning that discipline doesn't mean punishment — it means devotion.

For years, my energy was tied up in things that didn't deserve it. Family drama. Old narratives. Cycles that wanted attention more than they wanted healing.

I could've written a very different book from that place — one that might've sold well, gotten applause, or satisfied curiosity. But alignment asked me to choose substance over spectacle.

So, if you were waiting for a juicy exposé, I get it — but this season required something different from me. My focus changed. My intention matured. And I chose to pour into the family I created instead of staying stuck in the pain of the one I came from.

That choice gave me clarity. And clarity gave me stillness.

And before I make it sound like alignment erased all doubt, let me tell the truth: I deal with imposter syndrome — quietly, constantly, and sometimes convincingly.

There were moments while writing this book when I felt completely unprepared and unqualified to be doing it, like I had no business putting words together this way. Like somebody was going to tap me on the shoulder and say, *"Ma'am… we're gonna need you to step away from the keyboard."*

I questioned whether I was disciplined enough, focused enough, scholarly enough. I told myself I needed more time, more certainty, more credentials — more permission.

I almost failed before I even started.

Not because I couldn't write this book, but because imposter syndrome will have you trying to prove you belong instead of realizing you already do.

And I had to decide whether I was going to keep waiting to feel ready… or trust that growth happens after obedience.

I'm sharing this because I know what it feels like to be capable but unsupported, intelligent but uninformed, driven but exhausted. To be a mom, a wife, a student, a leader — and still figuring it out in real time.

Most women don't lack potential. They lack access, guidance, time, and honest examples.

People gatekeep knowledge for all kinds of reasons — fear, ego, scarcity, and insecurity. I don't believe in that.

Leaders   create   leaders.
Winners   make   winners.
And there is more than enough to go around.

We don't have to create money — it already exists. We just have to learn how to tap into the systems where it's already flowing by being grounded, focused, open-minded, and in alignment.

Let me say this clearly, especially if you're reading this thinking, *"She sounds confident — I'm not there yet."*

You   don't   have   to   be   rich.
You   don't   have   to   be   healed.
You   don't   have   to   be   perfect.
You don't even have to be sure. You just have to be willing.

Willing to think differently.
Willing to pause long enough to observe patterns.
Willing to build systems instead of surviving moments.
Willing to believe that your life can be designed — not just endured.

This book exists because I want women to feel like they have a friend in me. Not a guru. Not a motivator. Not someone yelling affirmations from a stage.

A woman who has lived, failed, adjusted, rebuilt, laughed, cursed, prayed, rested… and kept going.

My sister is the woman reading this — even if her life looks different, even if her struggles have different names.

So, if you've ever felt unseen, tired, capable, and still hopeful… this was written for you.

Now there you have it. Eight chapters. Not because everything is finished — but because this foundation is. What comes next will look different for each of us.

But if you take nothing else from this book, take this:

You   are   not   behind.
You   are   not   broken.
And you are not late.

You are becoming the woman you are meant to be, which doesn't require applause — it needs alignment.

So remember this, legacy isn't what people say about you. It's what continues to work after you stop explaining.

So,   build   wisely.
Rest   intentionally.
Share   generously.
And move forward — not from resentment, but from clarity.

That's what I'm doing now.

And if you're ready to do the same… welcome to the next cycle.

Just make sure you understand this:

You are designed — not desperate.